FISHING
with Cap'n Bob
and Matey

AN ENCYCLOPEDIA FOR KIDS OF ALL AGES

Illustrations by BOBBY BASNIGHT
Text by LEW HACKLER

SEASCAPE ENTERPRISES
Colonial Heights, VA, U.S.A.

NOTE: The glossary at the back contains many of the everyday words used by fishermen and those interested in the Great Outdoors. These words are intentionally given a very simple definition to make them easy to remember.

LIBRARY OF CONGRESS CATALOG CARD NUMBER 89-064309
ISBN 0-931595-05-3

Printed in Hong Kong by Everbest Printing Co. Ltd.
through Four Colour Imports, Ltd.

Distributed by THE TALMAN COMPANY

SEASCAPE ENTERPRISES
P.O. Box 176
Colonial Heights, VA 23834

DEDICATION

To my old fishing chums from Black River, Bugg's Island, Masonboro, Cape Hatteras, Wrightsville Beach, James River, Hampton Roads, Watauga Lake, Lake Murray, Tasman Sea, Bahamas, and the Outer Banks: Alan, Authur, Barney, Camm, Charles, Des, Dewey, Frank, George, Graham, Jere, Jim, Jimmy, Joe, Johnny, Levi, Parker, Percy, Pete, Poli, and Raymond. Many fond memories have been renewed doing this.

--L.H.

To my wife Shirley, who made life pleasant while I drew, and to Tom and Selina Stokes who know much about the sea.

--B.B.

Grateful acknowledgment is made to a champion, award-winning sportfisherman, Dr. Parker Moore, boating companion and friend, for checking the Glossary. Thanks also to both Cap'n Earl Dye and Jim Fulmer, both award-winning fishermen, boatsmen, and lovers of The Great Outdoors, for their valuable suggestions; and to Patricia Rychlik Blaszak for her good advice and editing.

Wow! That's a BRAGGING-SIZE fish this ANGLER just hooked. Too bad he's got a BACKLASH and may lose it.

Better luck next time!

Matey likes all this ACTION. It's exciting, and the fish are BITING on both BLOODWORMS and ARTIFICIAL LURES.

A

Cap'n Bob is cooking the lunch he caught. "Ummmm! Ummmm! That smells good. Woozy, do you like the AROMA?" he asks.

When you go fishing, it's a good idea to watch the others to see what kind of BOTTOM RIG and BAIT they are using, and what kind of fish they're catching.

Let's go see what we can catch.

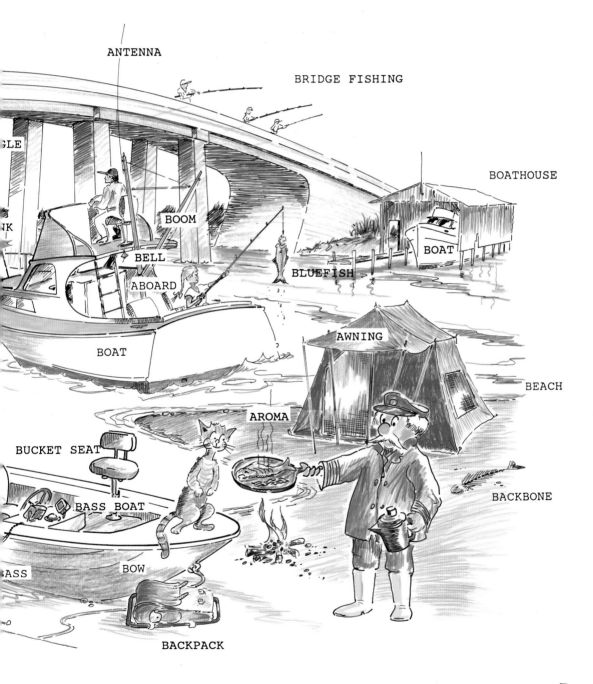

Cap'n Bob caught some trouble, its seems, and is getting a CITATION for the little fish. His EXCUSE for keeping such a little one for bait didn't work with this Game Warden.

Woozy is hiding her CATCH. Cats will do just about anything for a fish dinner, and Woozy is no exception.

Ted is DRESSING OUT a nice CATFISH. It will be the best fish dinner, one he CAUGHT, CLEANED, and COOKED over his very own CAMPFIRE.

If you don't CATCH even one fish it is still a great EXPERIENCE just to be outside, enjoying nature.

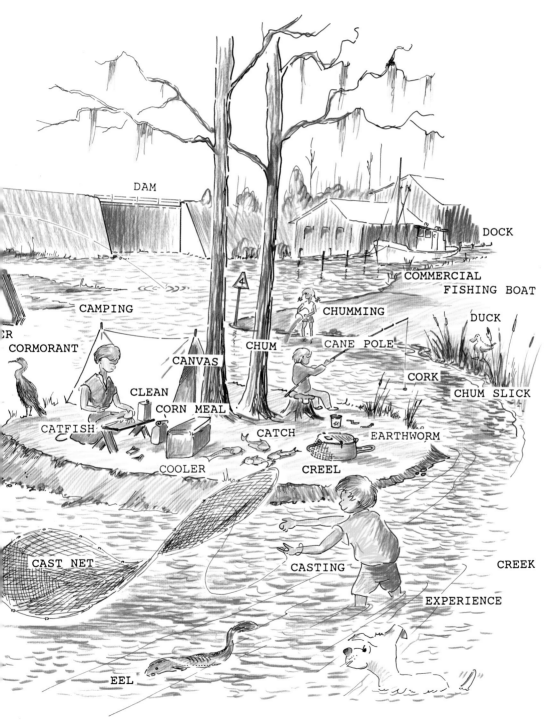

DAM

DOCK

COMMERCIAL
FISHING BOAT

CAMPING

CHUMMING

DUCK

CR
CORMORANT

CHUM

CANE POLE

CANVAS

CORK

CHUM SLICK

CLEAN

CORN MEAL

CATFISH

CATCH

EARTHWORM

COOLER

CREEL

CAST NET

CASTING

CREEK

EXPERIENCE

EEL

"That big!" declares Cap'n Bob, as he tells a FISH STORY about his FIGHT with the big catch FRYING in the FRYING PAN.

"Our GUIDE really knew where to go."

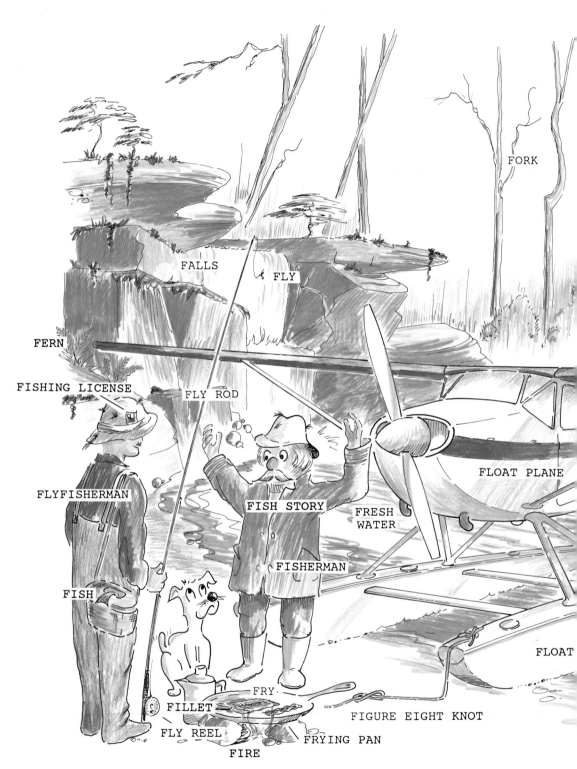

FORK

FALLS

FLY

FERN

FISHING LICENSE

FLY ROD

FLOAT PLANE

FLYFISHERMAN

FISH STORY

FRESH WATER

FISHERMAN

FISH

FLOAT

FRY

FILLET

FIGURE EIGHT KNOT

FLY REEL

FRYING PAN

FIRE

F

"This fishing is great", says the FLYFISHERMAN. "Just be sure you have your FISHING LICENSE. I was checked by the GAME WARDEN, and he is coming this way."

FLOCK

GEESE

FLAG

EAT OUTDOORS

FLAGPOLE

FISHING LODGE

GILLS

GUIDE

FISHING TACKLE

GAFF   GIG

FLATHEAD CATFISH

FLOAT

FIN

FISHING POLE

GUNWALE (GUNNEL)

FREEBOARD

RD

GAR

FISH

GRUB WORM

FISHING HOLE

G

The HELMSMAN always knows where the HOT SPOTS are, and today they're really HITTING! Just about all are KEEPERS, too.

Cap'n Bob says, "Matey, it's all in KNOWING WHERE TO GO."

"Here comes another one!"

Cap'n Bob doesn't need a license for saltwater fishing on a HEADBOAT, and the boat has everything he needs except an ICE CHEST to put his catch in.

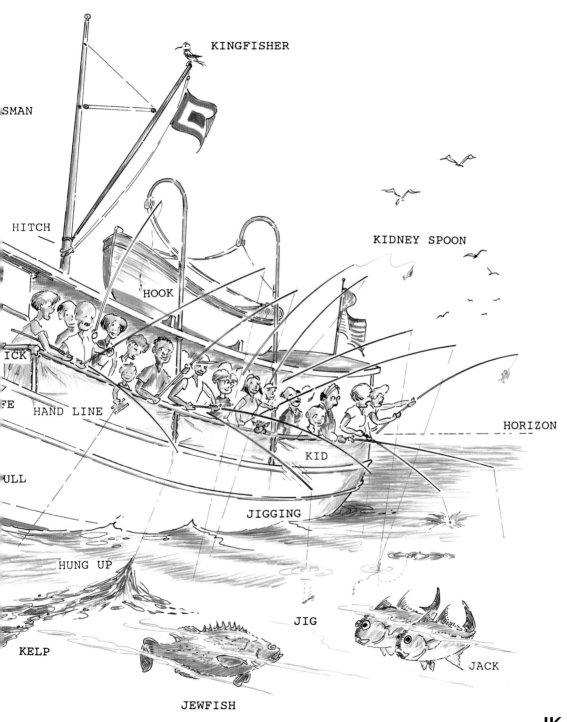

KINGFISHER

SMAN

KIDNEY SPOON

HITCH

HOOK

ICK

FE
HAND LINE

HORIZON

KID

ULL

JIGGING

HUNG UP

JIG

KELP

JACK

JEWFISH

JK

Matey's keeping a eye on the LOBSTERS. The claws look like they can bite!

"Stand by to catch the MOORING BUOY," yells the Cap'n. "I'm slowing down."

"Easy, Cap'n" replies the LOOKOUT. "We're almost there, but watch out for the red NUN. Do you see it?"

NAVIGATION LIGHT

LEADHEAD

NAVIGATION CHARTS

LURE

LEADER

LIGHTHOUSE

MIRROR SMOOTH

LICENSE

MUSSEL

LOBSTER

BASNight

The MATE is collecting LIVE BAIT out of the NET for some NIGHT FISHING by the LIGHTHOUSE.

Woozy would surely like to have just one of the MINNOWS for a little snack right now, but her chance will come later.

Woozy is thinking we LANDED a good catch today. Another great day enjoying NATURE.

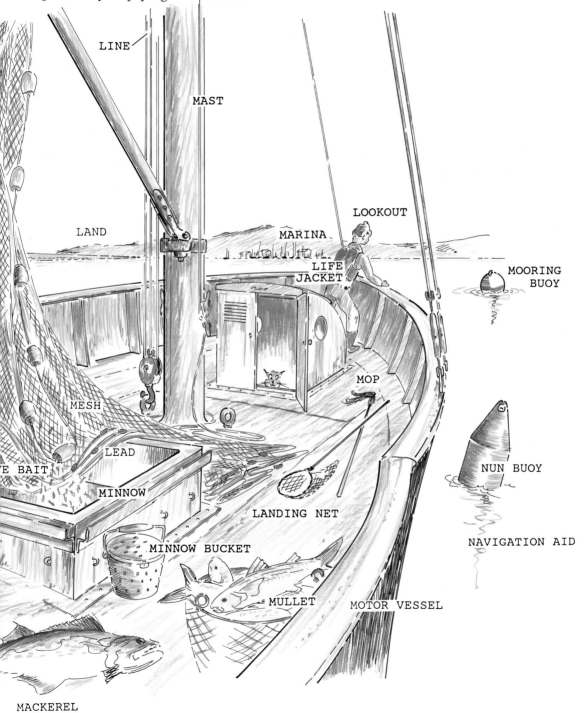

LINE

MAST

LOOKOUT

LAND

MARINA

LIFE JACKET

MOORING BUOY

MOP

MESH

LEAD

NUN BUOY

E BAIT

MINNOW

LANDING NET

NAVIGATION AID

MINNOW BUCKET

MULLET

MOTOR VESSEL

MACKEREL

"Darn," Cap'n Bob grumbles. "I must report the OIL POLLUTION to someone to get it stopped. It is ruining our OYSTER beds".

"I wish everyone would help keep our OCEANS, rivers, and PONDS clean. They are special treasures for us and for future generations to use and enjoy."

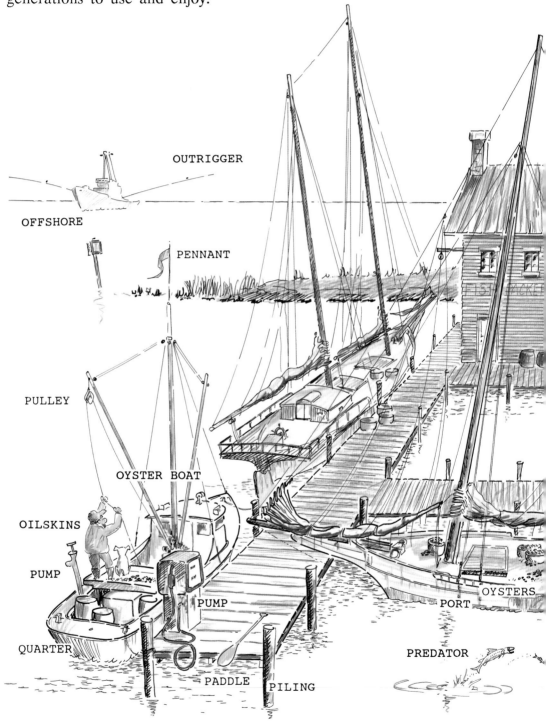

OUTRIGGER

OFFSHORE

PENNANT

PULLEY

OYSTER BOAT

OILSKINS

PUMP

PUMP

QUARTER

PADDLE

PILING

OYSTERS

PORT

PREDATOR

O

Sometimes PIER FISHING takes a lot of PATIENCE, but it's paying off today, except for the fish Woozy sneaked off with.

"Come back here Woozy! You can have the bones after supper," says Sue.

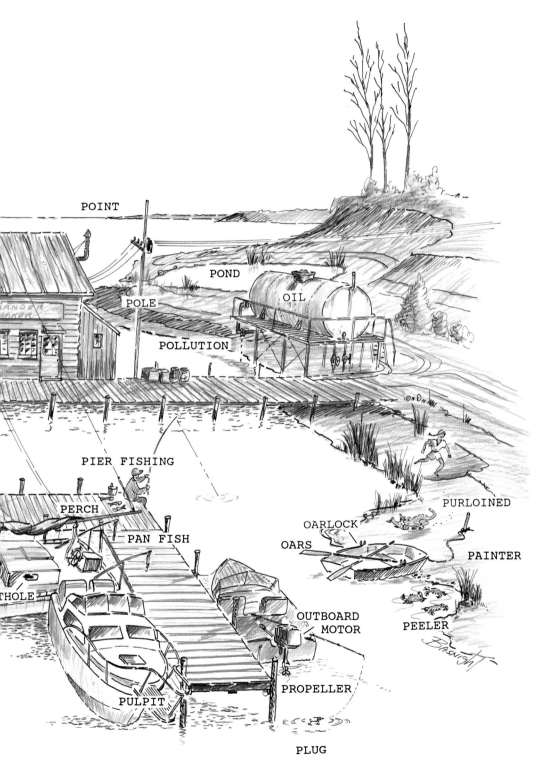

POINT
POND
POLE
OIL
POLLUTION
PIER FISHING
PERCH
PAN FISH
CHOLE
OARLOCK
OARS
PURLOINED
PAINTER
OUTBOARD MOTOR
PEELER
PULPIT
PROPELLER
PLUG

The SURFCASTER has one fish on his STRINGER, and Matey barks at a SCHOOL swimming offshore.

The SEA is warm, and the divers are going SPEARFISHING on the REEF. The should have good luck because fish are everywhere today. Just keep an eye on that STORM.

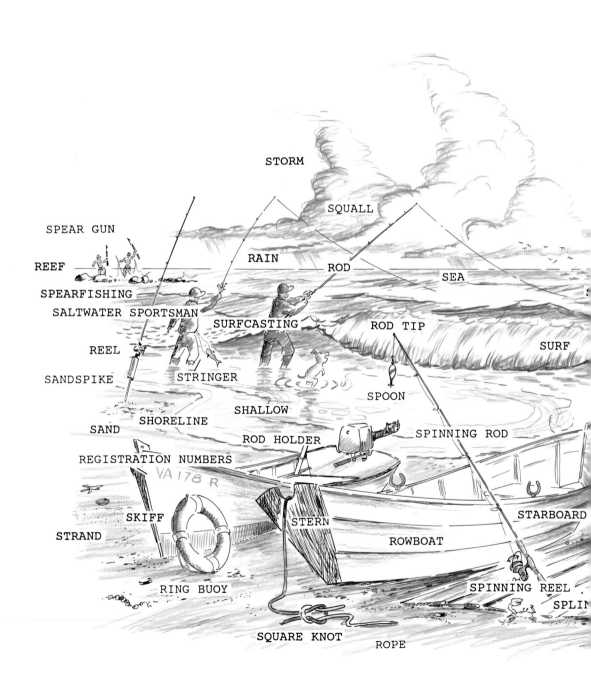

STRIKE!

When the SAILFISH hit, Cap'n Bob was talking to the SKIPPER of the SPORTFISHERMAN on the RADIO.

"Not a RECORD, but not bad," he said. "Boy, what a SPORT!"

"Now, SET THE HOOK, slow the boat down, and don't REEL IN too fast. Don't give him any SLACK," yells Cap'n Bob.

"That's a fine catch, but I hope you RELEASE it for someone else to catch another day."

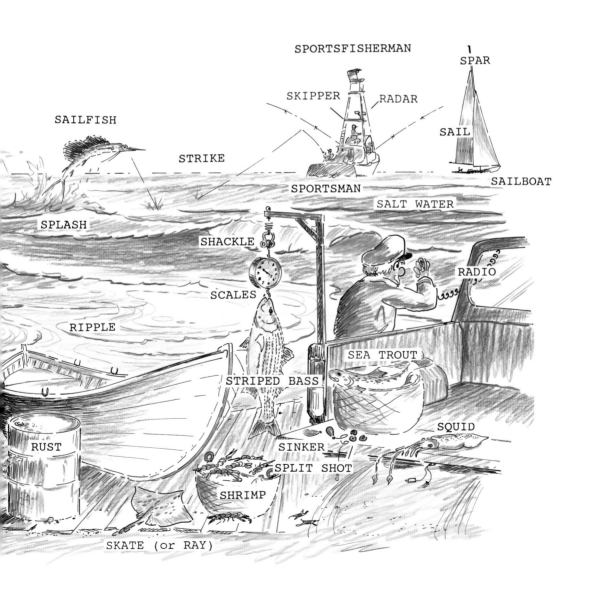

SPORTSFISHERMAN

SPAR

SKIPPER   RADAR

SAILFISH

SAIL

STRIKE

SAILBOAT

SPORTSMAN

SALT WATER

SPLASH

SHACKLE

RADIO

SCALES

RIPPLE

SEA TROUT

STRIPED BASS

SQUID

RUST

SINKER

SPLIT SHOT

SHRIMP

SKATE (or RAY)

S

Mike's Dad said, "This is THE ONE THAT GOT AWAY. Too bad! It would have been big enough to win a TROPHY, too."

"Come on Dad", says Mike. "We've got to rescue Woozy! She didn't notice the TIDE changed, and it caused the boat to swing away."

The U.S. COAST GUARD wouldn't like to find Mike in such an UNSAFE place, especially without his lifejacket!

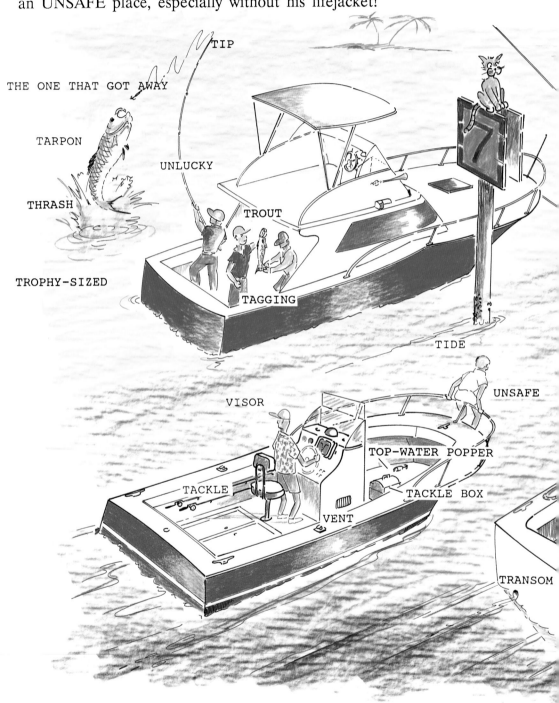

"I hope that THORNBACK RAY doesn't bite my hook." says Sue. "We caught a nice VARIETY today, but we do not need that one!"

Poor Cap'n Bob is thinking about cleaning all the fish, especially the UNDERSIZED ones. Maybe this would be a good day to teach Ted how to clean fish. Next time he'll remember to put the little ones back so they can grow bigger.

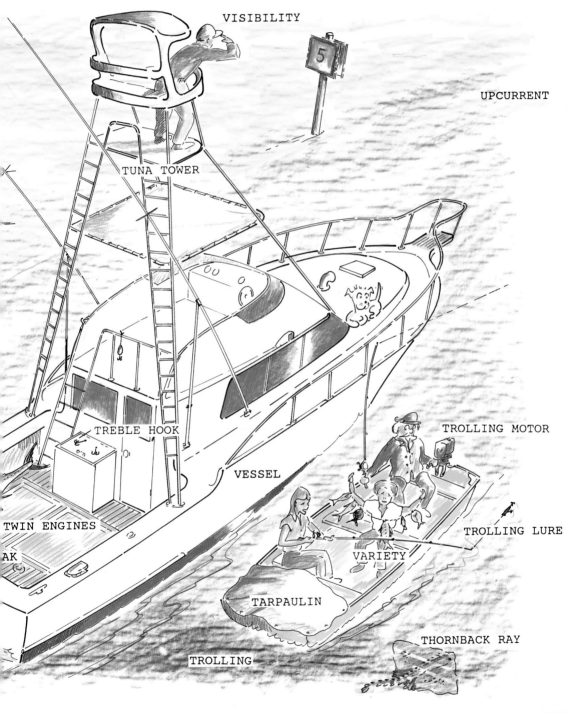

VISIBILITY

UPCURRENT

TUNA TOWER

TREBLE HOOK

TROLLING MOTOR

VESSEL

TWIN ENGINES

AK

TROLLING LURE

VARIETY

TARPAULIN

THORNBACK RAY

TROLLING

UV

"The WIND is blowing harder, Matey," says Cap'n Bob. "You can see the WAVES building, and the cat is beginning to look a little WOOZY."

"I can feel the WIND-CHILL on my nose, and the fish have stopped biting."

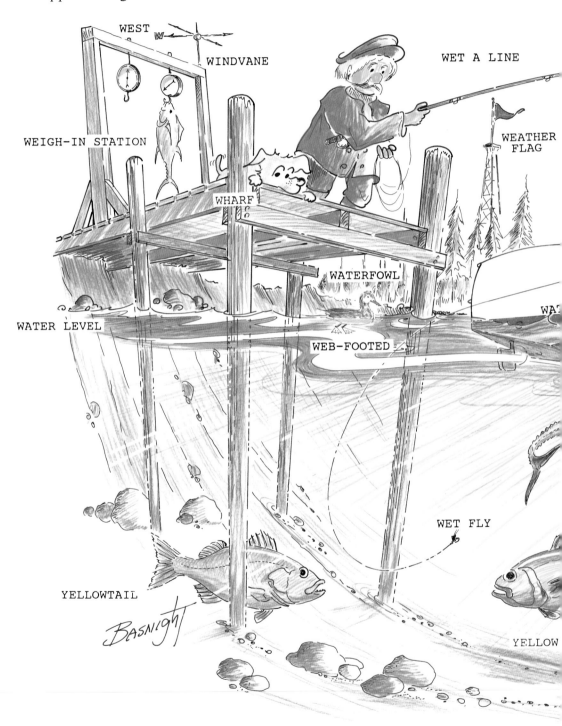

WEST
WINDVANE
WEIGH-IN STATION
WHARF
WET A LINE
WEATHER FLAG
WATERFOWL
WATER LEVEL
WEB-FOOTED
WA
WET FLY
YELLOWTAIL
YELLOW
BASNIGHT

Cap'n Bob says, "When you go WET A LINE", try to keep warm and stay dry. But the two most important things are to keep a lookout for changes in the WEATHER, and always remember, *SAFETY FIRST*."

GOOD LUCK TO YOU, WHEN YOU GO FISHING!

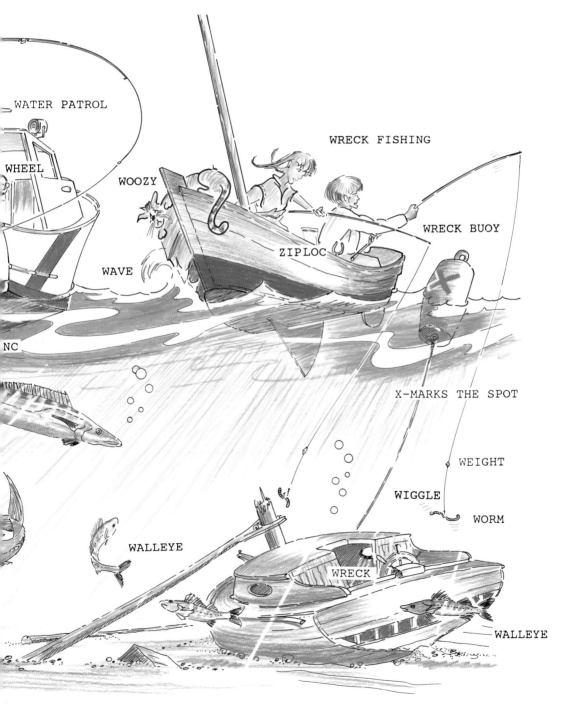

WATER PATROL

WHEEL

WOOZY

WAVE

NC

WRECK FISHING

ZIPLOC

WRECK BUOY

X-MARKS THE SPOT

WEIGHT

WIGGLE

WORM

WALLEYE

WRECK

WALLEYE

GLOSSARY OF FISHING TERMS

ABOARD - On a boat.
ACTION - (1) When fish are biting. (2) Getting a nibble.
ANCHOR - A heavy metal object that keeps boats from drifting.
ANGLER - Anyone who fishes with a pole or rod.
ANTENNA - A skinny rod or wire connected to a radio which sends or receives messages.
AROMA - A very special smell that is easy to notice.
ARTIFICIAL LURE - A man-made bait used to fool fish.
ASHORE - On the shore. Not on a boat.
AWNING - A canvas roof or sunshade.

BACKBONE - The bony spine down the middle of a fish.
BACKLASH - When fishing line gets tangled on a reel.
BACKPACK - A camping bag held on your back with straps.
BAIT - Anything used on a hook (or in a trap) to catch fish.
BAIT BUCKET - A bucket used to hold bait.
BALD EAGLE - The national bird of the United States of America.
BALLYHOO - A small shiny fish used for bait.
BANK - The raised ground next to a body of water.

Bait (rigged for fishing)

BARB - A raised burr on a hook to keep fish from getting off.
BASS - A very popular game fish; fun to catch and good to eat.
BASS BOAT - A fast boat made for fishing on fresh water.
BATEAU - A small flat-bottomed boat, squared off on each end.
BATTERY - A heavy box or case that holds electricity.
BEACH - The sandy shore of an ocean, lake, or river.
BEACON - A signal light used to help guide boats and airplanes.
BELL - A hollow metal bowl that rings when struck.
BILLFISH - A fish with long jaws. Marlin, sailfish, swordfish.

BINOCULARS - Used to make far-off things look close.
BITING - Time when fish are being caught on hooks.
BLOODWORM - A worm with red juice inside that is used for bait.
BLUEFISH - A kind of fish caught in saltwater.
BOAT - A small vessel that is moved by oars, sails or engine.
BOATHOUSE - A building to keep boats in.
BOOM - A pole that holds out the foot (bottom) of a sail.
BOTTOM FISHING - Fishing with the hook on the bottom.

Billfish

BOTTOM RIG - The hooks, weights and things fastened together for bottom fishing.
BOW - The forward (front) part of a boat.
BOW RAIL - The front railing on a boat.
BRAGGING-SIZE - A fish big enough to make other people wish they had caught it.
BRIDGE - (1) A structure that lets you cross over water. (2) The top deck on some boats.
BRIDGE FISHING - Fishing from a bridge that crosses over water.
BUCKET SEAT - A seat with a rounded back.
BUCKTAIL - An imitation bait with feather or hair and a hook.
BUOY - A floating marker.

CAMOUFLAGE - A way to hide things and make them hard to see.
CAMPFIRE - Outdoor fire used to keep warm and to cook food.
CANE POLE - A fishing pole made from a bamboo shoot.
CANOE - A long boat pointed at both ends that is easy to paddle.
CANVAS - (1) Cloth used for tents or on boats. (2) Sails.
CAPTAIN - The person who gives orders on a boat. The boss.
CARP - A kind of freshwater fish.
CASTING - Throwing a fishing line or net into the water.
CAST NET - A small net that can be thrown to catch things.
CATCH - (1) To capture. (2) "The Catch" is all the fish caught.
CATFISH - A kind of fish with whiskers.
CAUGHT - When you have really landed a fish.
CHANNEL MARKER - Used to mark the safe edges of a channel.
CHART - A map used to find your way on the water.
CHARTER BOAT - A boat you pay to go out on.
CHUM - (1) A pal. (2) Ground up fish food. Makes fish active.
CHUMMING - Throwing chum into the water.
CHUM SLICK - The oil and bits of fish food that float.
CITATION - (1) An award for catching a large fish. (2) A ticket for doing something that's against the law.

CLAMPS - Jaws which have a spring in them to squeeze things.
CLEAN - To remove fish scales and parts you don't want to eat.
COMMERCIAL FISHING BOAT - Used for fishing to earn a living.
COMPASS - Helps show the direction by always pointing north.
COOK - Using heat to fix food and make it taste good.
COOLER - Insulated container used to keep things in.
CORK - Keeps a hook from sinking. Bobbles when a fish nibbles.
CORMORANT - A kind of bird seen around water.
CORN MEAL - Ground up corn that is used for cooking.
CRAPPIE - A kind of fish that is fun to catch and good to eat. Freckle.
CREEK - A stream of water that is smaller than a river.
CREEL - A small basket with a carry-strap to keep fish in.
CRICKET CAN - Keeps crickets alive to use for bait.
CYPRESS TREE - A kind of tree that grows in or near water.

DAM - Used to hold water back. It usually makes a lake.
DANFORTH ANCHOR - A special lightweight anchor.
DEPTH FINDER - Measures how deep the water is under a boat.
DIP NET - A net with a handle. Used to get fish into a boat.
DOLPHIN - (1) A kind of fish that is fun to catch and good to eat.
Mahi Mahi. Dorado. (2) A mammal; not a fish. Porpoise.
DRAG - To slip some. Not fixed.
DRESS OUT - To clean fish.
DRY FLY - An artificial bait that floats
and looks like a fly.
DUCK - (1) A kind of bird that swims. (2)
A quick body movement to keep from
being hit by something.

Dolphin (mammal)

EARTHWORM - A skinny worm that
wiggles and makes good bait.
EEL - A skinny fish that looks something like a snake.
ELECTRIC MOTOR - A small quiet motor that runs on electricity.
ENGINE - A mechanical device used to put a boat in motion.
EXCUSE - Trying to explain why something isn't right.
EXPERIENCE - Knowing how to do things by doing them.

FALLS - A waterfall. Water coming down from somewhere higher.
FEEDING - When fish are eating and looking for more food to eat.
FIGHT - The struggle between a fisherman and a fish on a hook.
FIGURE EIGHT KNOT - Sometimes used at the end of a line.
FILLET - A piece of fish with the bones removed.
FIN - The wings on the top, bottom, sides or tail of a fish.
FIRE - Something burning.

FISH - A creature that lives in water and has fins and gills.
FISH STORY - Making things seem like more than they really were.
FISHERMAN - Anyone who fishes with a pole, net, gig, or trap.
FISHING HOLE - A place known to be good for fishing.

Dolphin (fish)

FISHING LICENSE - A permit to fish.
FISHING LODGE - A place for fishermen to stay in.
FISHING POLE - A pole with a hook and line used to catch fish.
FISHING TACKLE - All the things used to go fishing.
FLAG - A colored rectangular cloth with a special meaning.
FLAGPOLE - A pole used to fly a flag.
FLATHEAD CATFISH - Kind of fish; fun to catch and good to eat.
FLOAT - To sit on the water. Not to sink.
FLOAT PLANE - An airplane made to land and take off on water.
FLOCK - A group of birds or animals that stay together.
FLY - (1) To go into the sky. (2) A small artificial bait.
FLY LINE - The fishing line used on a fly rod.
FLY REEL - A spool used to wind up a fly line.
FLY ROD - A special kind of fishing rod used for fly casting.
FLYFISHERMAN - A fisherman who uses a fly rod and a fly.
FORK - Where the parts separate like the top of a "Y".
FORWARD - Toward the bow (toward the front) of a boat.
FREEBOARD - The height from the waterline to the deck.
FRESH WATER - Not salt water.
FRY - (1) To cook in hot oil. (2) Baby fish.
FRYING PAN - A big flat pan with a handle used for frying.

Fly

GAFF - A hook on a handle used for lifting heavy fish.
GAME WARDEN - A person in uniform who checks on fishing laws.
GAR - A long freshwater fish; not good to eat.
GEESE - More than one goose. A kind of waterfowl.
GIG - A spear with prongs used to catch fish.
GILLS - Slits on the side of a fish's head used for breathing.
GREAT OUTDOORS - Being out in Nature.
GRUB WORM - A fat worm used for bait.
GUIDE - (1) An eyelet. (2) Person who is paid to lead others.
GUNWALE (GUNNEL) - The top of the boat's sides. The rail.

HADDOCK - A kind of saltwater fish that is good to eat. Cod.
HALIBUT - A kind of fish that is good to eat. Flounder. Sole.
HAMMERHEAD - A shark with eyes at the edges of a flat head.
HAND LINE - A fishing line used without a reel.
HAND RAIL - A wooden or metal rail to hold onto.
HARBOR - A safe place for a boat.
HARPOON - Spear with a barb used to catch big fish and whales.
HEAD BOAT - Charges people so much money a head to go fishing.
HELM - A tiller or wheel used to steer a boat.
HELMSMAN - Person who steers a boat.
HITCH - A loop around an object then back around itself.
HITTING - When the fish are biting.
HOOK - A curved metal wire with a barb used to catch fish.
HORIZON - Where the earth (or sea) and sky seem to meet.
HORN - Used to make special sound signals to bridges and boats.
HOT SPOT - A really good place to catch fish.
HULL - The body of a boat or ship.
HUNG UP - When a hook or line gets caught on something.

ICE CHEST - A container for keeping things cold and fresh.
ICE PICK - A very sharp spike with a handle used to chip ice.
INBOARD - (1) Within a boat. (2) A boat with a built-in engine.
ISLAND - A body of land surrounded by water.

JACK - A kind of saltwater fish; fun to catch and good to eat.
JEWFISH - A large saltwater fish; very good to eat. Grouper.
JIG - A kind of fishing lure used for jigging.
JIGGING - Fishing with short little jerks on the line.

Lure

KEEL - The underwater backbone on the bottom of a boat.
KEEPER - Any fish large enough to keep for eating.
KELP - A kind of seaweed. Fish like to swim under it.
KIDNEY SPOON - A fishing lure with an oval shape.
KIDS - Young people.
KING MACKEREL - A kind of saltwater fish; good to eat. Kingfish.
KINGFISHER - A kind of bird (waterfowl) seen around water.
KNIFE - A sharp blade with a handle used to cut things.
KNOT - A tie point.
KNOWING WHERE TO GO - The good places to catch fish.

LAND - (1) To get a fish into the boat. (2) The shore.
LANDED - Gotten out of the water.
LANDING NET - A net with a handle used to get fish into a boat.
LANTERN - A light that doesn't have to be plugged in.
LARGEMOUTH BASS - Puts up a big fight and is good to eat.
LEAD - (1) A heavy metal weight. (2) To be first.
LEADER - (1) A strong wire or string used between a lure and the fishing line. (2) The person in charge.
LEADHEAD - A kind of heavy artificial bait.
LEAK - Any hole or crack that lets water in.
LICENSE - A permit that is needed to do something.
LIFE JACKET - Keeps a person floating in the water.
LIGHTHOUSE - A building with a strong light that guides ships.
LINE - (1) The string used to catch fish. (2) Rope on a boat.
LINE-TWIST - Causes line to kink up because of too much twist.
LIVE BAIT - Natural, live things that fish like to eat.
LOBSTER - A shellfish that is very good to eat.
LOOKOUT - Someone assigned to look for something.
LURE - Something used to tempt fish to bite.

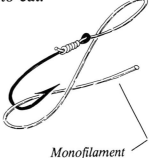
Monofilament

MACKEREL - A kind of fish; fun to catch and good to eat.
MARINA - A place on water that keeps boats and sells supplies.
MARLIN - A kind of billfish; fun to catch but not good to eat.
MAST - A tall spar (pole) that supports sails.
MATE - (1) Someone on a boat that helps. (2) A pal.
MESH - The opening between strings in a net.
MINNOW - A very small fish, sometimes called Shiners.
MINNOW BUCKET - A special bucket for keeping live minnows in.
MIRROR SMOOTH - Water smooth enough to see yourself in.
MONO (MONOFILAMENT) - A solid plastic line with no strands.
MOORING BUOY - A float with a heavy anchor to tie a boat to.
MOP - Used to swab the decks, and keep them clean.
MOTOR VESSEL - A boat propelled by an engine. A motorboat.
MUSSEL - A shellfish with two shells that close together.
MULLET - A kind of oily fish; good for bait or can be eaten.

NATURE - All the critters and things in The Great Outdoors.
NAVIGATION AIDS - Lights, buoys, and markers with special meanings that help boats stay safe and find their way.
NAVIGATION CHART - A kind of map used on boats.
NAVIGATION LIGHT - Used to help boats find their way at night.

NET - A web that water goes through used to catch things.
NETTLE - A kind of sea creature with tentacles that can sting.
NIGHT FISHING - Fishing at night.
NUN BUOY - A floating marker pointed at the top.

OARLOCK - A U-shaped holder that keeps an oar in place.
OARS - A long pole with a blade used to row or steer a boat.
OCEAN - A great body of water between continents.
OFFSHORE - In the ocean, out of the sight of land.
OIL - A fuel or lubricant needed to make things work, but if spilled it floats on water and kills fish.
OILSKINS - Waterproof clothing also called foul-weather gear.
OUTBOARD MOTOR - A removable engine for boats.
OUTRIGGER - Long poles to hold trolling lines out to the side.
OYSTER - A shellfish with irregular shells that close together.
OYSTER BOAT - A kind of boat used for collecting oysters.

PADDLE - A short light pole with a blade at one end and a handle at the other. Used to paddle or steer a boat.
PAINTER - A line (rope) tied to the bow of a boat.
PAN FISH - The size fish that just fits inside a frying pan.
PEELER - A crab with a very soft shell. Makes good bait.
PERCH - A kind of fish, fun to catch and good to eat.
PIER - A platform that goes from the land out into the water.
PIER FISHING - Fishing from a pier.
PILING (PILE) - A pole driven into the ground underwater.
PLASTIC WORM - A flexible, colored, plastic worm with hooks.

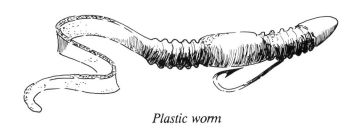

Plastic worm

PLUG - An artificial bait used to catch fish. A lure.
POINT - Where land sticks out into a body of water.
POLE - Any kind of long rod, or spar.
POLLUTION - Trash, garbage or chemicals turned loose in Nature.
POND - A small lake.
PORT - (1) The left side of a boat when you face forward; (2) a small round window; (3) a harbor where boats usually go.
PORTHOLE - A small round window. A port.

PREDATOR - Catches and feeds on other animals.
PREY - Something being hunted to be eaten.
PROPELLER - A blade that spins to move boats and planes.
PULLEY - A grooved wheel for line, wire or rope. It changes the direction of the rope.
PULPIT - A strong guardrail around the bow or stern.
PUMP - A device used to remove water or other liquids.
PURLOINED - Stolen.

QUARTER - Either side of a boat's stern.

RADAR - Uses radio waves to "see" and help you find the way.
RADIO - Uses radio waves to help you talk to others.
RAIN - Water droplets falling from the sky.
RAMP - A roadway into the water for launching or loading boats.
RAY - A kind of fish, flat and shaped like a diamond.
RECORD - Better (or bigger) than done before.
REEF - An underwater ledge that sticks up from the bottom.
REEL - (1) A spool to wind line on. (2) Winding the line up.
REGISTRATION NUMBERS - The license for a boat.
RELEASE - Letting a live fish loose to swim away.
RING BUOY - A float that can be thrown to someone in the water.
RIPPLE - A tiny little wave.
ROD - A fishing pole with eyes for line to pass through.
ROD HOLDER - Anything used to hold a fishing rod in place.
ROD TIP - The eye at the end of a fishing pole.
ROPE - Is called Line when used on a boat.
ROWBOAT - A small boat made for rowing.
RUST - Metal that turns to brown dust and starts to fall apart.

SAFETY FIRST - Being very careful in everything you do.
SAIL - A cloth that catches the wind to push a boat.
SAILBOAT - A boat that uses sails to make it move.
SAILFISH - A billfish that gives a big fight. Not good to eat.
SALT WATER - Ocean water. It has salt and many other minerals.
SALTWATER SPORTSMAN - Someone who usually fishes in salt water.
SAND - Tiny grains of rock, about the size of salt.
SAND FIDDLER - A small ocean animal that digs into the sand.
SAND SPIKE - Sticks into the sand to hold a fishing pole.
SCALES - (1) Small flakes on the skin of many fish. (2) Used to see how much something weighs.
SCHOOL - A group of fish swimming together.
SEA - (1) The ocean or big body of water. (2) A large wave.
SEA TROUT - A kind of fish that is good to eat.

SET THE HOOK - Giving a quick tug so the fish gets caught.
SHACKLE - A U-shaped metal fitting with a pin across the "U".
SHALLOW - Where the water is not very deep.
SHARP - A point or blade that can stick or cut very easily.
SHORELINE - Along the edge of the water. The shore.
SHRIMP - A small sea animal, good to eat and good for bait.
SINKER - A weight used to sink a fishing line (or a net).
SKATE - A kind of flat fish shaped like a diamond. A Ray.
SKIFF - A light rowboat.
SKIMMER - A bird that skims over water to catch food.
SKIPPER - The Captain. The person in charge.
SLACK - Loose. Not tight.
SNAG - Caught on something. (See front cover)
SNAP SWIVEL - A metal wire clip with a swivel.
SPAR - A pole.

Sharp

SPEAR GUN - Used to shoot a spear underwater.
SPEARFISHING - Diving underwater to spear (shoot) fish.
SPINNER - A small blade that spins when it moves through water.
SPINNING REEL - Line comes off over the end of the reel.
SPINNING ROD - A rod made to be used with a spinning reel.
SPLASH - To plop into the water.

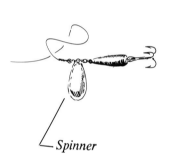

Spinner

SPLINTER - A small, sharp piece of wood.
SPLIT SHOT - Small weights to squeeze onto a fishing line.
SPOON - A shiny rounded metal lure.
SPORT - (1) An activity to enjoy. (2) A person that plays fair.
SPORTSFISHERMAN - (1) A boat with a flying bridge and an open cockpit. (2) Someone who fishes for sport.

SPORTSMAN - Someone who treats fishing (or hunting) fairly.
SQUALL - A sudden storm with wind and rain.
SQUARE KNOT - A double knot. Also called a reef knot.
SQUID - A sea animal with tentacles. Good bait and good to eat.
STARBOARD - The right side of a boat.
STERN - The aft (rear) part of the boat.
STORM - Bad weather with strong wind and rain.
STRAND - A beach by the water.
STRIKE - Hit, like when a fish hits the bait.
STRINGER - A cord or chain to keep caught fish on.
STRIPED BASS - A fish that gives a big fight. Good to eat.
SURF - The waves breaking on a beach.
SURFCASTING - Casting out into the ocean from the shore.
SWIVEL - Lets a line spin without twisting it up.

TACKLE - All poles, lures, and lines to fish with.
TACKLE BOX - A box to keep fishing things in.
TAGGING - Catching, identifying and releasing a fish.
TARPAULIN - A heavy cloth cover to protect things.
TARPON - A kind of fish that puts up a real fight.
TAXIDERMIST - Someone who knows how to stuff a trophy.
TEAK - A kind of wood used on boats.
TERMINAL TACKLE - The hooks and sinker on the end of a line.
THE ONE THAT GOT AWAY - The big fish we wish we had caught.
THRASH - Tossing, flipping, and splashing.
THORNBACK RAY - A wide flat fish with a stinger on its back.
TIDE - The rise and fall of sea water height.

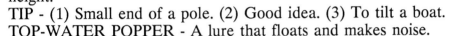

Treble hook

TIP - (1) Small end of a pole. (2) Good idea. (3) To tilt a boat.
TOP-WATER POPPER - A lure that floats and makes noise.
TRANSOM - The stern (rear) surface of a boat.
TREBLE HOOK - Three hooks made together.
TROLLING - Fishing behind a moving boat.
TROLLING LURE - A fishing lure used while trolling.
TROLLING MOTOR - A small, quiet, outboard motor.
TROPHY - (1) A prize award. (2) A mounted fish to hang up.
TROPHY-SIZE - A good size to be mounted as a trophy.
TROUT - A kind of fish fun to catch and good to eat.
TUNA - A large saltwater fish, fun to catch and good to eat.
TUNA TOWER - A high platform used to see far off over water.
TWIN ENGINES - Has two engines the same size.

UNLUCKY - Missing out on catching the fish we wanted.
UNSAFE - Something that could cause someone to get hurt.
UPCURRENT - Going against the flow of water.
U.S.C.G. VESSEL - A United States Coast Guard vessel.

VARIETY - All different kinds. Not the same.
VENT - Used to get fresh air below decks.
VESSEL - Any boat or ship.
VISIBILITY - Just how far you can see on land or water.
VISOR - A open hat with a front brim to shade eyes.

WAHOO - A kind of fish that gives a big fight. Good to eat.
WALLEYE - A kind of fish that gives a big fight. Good to eat.
WATER LEVEL - The actual height of the water.

WATER PATROL - Officials that enforce laws around water.
WATERFOWL - Kinds of birds that live around water.
WATERLINE - The water level on a boat's hull.
WAVE - A swell moving across the water.
WEATHER - General conditions, but usually means bad weather.
WEATHER FLAG - Signal flags used to tell the weather forecast.
WEB-FOOTED - Animals with webs between their toes to swim with.
WEIGH-IN STATION - An official place to weigh fish.
WEIGHT - (1) Something used to sink a fishing line. (2) How much something weighs.
WEST - The general direction the sun sets in.
WET A LINE - Go fishing.
WET FLY - An artificial bait that looks like a fly and sinks.
WHARF - A place to bring bigger boats or ships alongside.
WHEEL - Can be turned to steer something with.
WIGGLE - Moving back and forth.
WIND - Moving air.
WIND-CHILL - Coldness felt when the wind blows.
WINDVANE - An arrow that points towards the wind.
WOOZY - When your head feels like it's spinning.
WORM - A long wiggly bug. Good bait for catching fish.
WRECK - The remains of a sunken boat.
WRECK BUOY - Used to mark the location of a wreck.
WRECK FISHING - Fishing near a wreck.

X-MARKS-THE-SPOT - A certain location for something.

YELLOW JACK - A kind of fish fun to catch and good to eat.
YELLOWTAIL - Also fun to catch and good to eat.

ZINC - A chunk of metal used to protect boat parts.
ZIPLOC - A kind of plastic bag that you can snap shut.